SONIA SOTOMAYOR

THE SUPREME COURT'S FIRST HISPANIC JUSTICE

RICHARD BARRINGTON

Britannica
Educational Publishing

IN ASSOCIATION WITH

ROSEN
EDUCATIONAL SERVICES

Published in 2015 by Britannica Educational Publishing (a trademark of Encyclopædia Britannica, Inc.)
in association with The Rosen Publishing Group, Inc.
29 East 21st Street, New York, NY 10010

Distributed exclusively by Rosen Publishing.
To see additional Britannica Educational Publishing titles, go to rosenpublishing.com.

First Edition

Britannica Educational Publishing
J.E. Luebering: Director, Core Reference Group
Anthony L. Green: Editor, Compton's by Britannica

Rosen Publishing
Hope Lourie Killcoyne: Executive Editor
Shalini Saxena: Editor
Nelson Sá: Art Director
Brian Garvey: Designer
Cindy Reiman: Photography Manager
Marty Levick: Photo Research

Cataloging-in-Publication Data

Barrington, Richard, 1961- , author.
Sonia Sotomayor: the Supreme Court's first Hispanic justice/Richard Barrington.—First edition.
    pages cm.—(Making a difference: leaders who are changing the world)
Includes bibliographical references and index.
ISBN 978-1-62275-435-9 (library bound)—ISBN 978-1-62275-437-3 (pbk.)—
ISBN 978-1-62275-438-0 (6-pack)
1. Sotomayor, Sonia, 1954—Juvenile literature. 2. Judges—United States—Biography—Juvenile
literature. 3. United States. Supreme Court—Biography—Juvenile literature. I. Title.
KF8745.S67B37 2015
347.73'2634—dc23
[B]
                                                2014002022

Manufactured in the United States of America.

Photo credits: Cover, p. 1 © iStockphoto.com/EdStock; cover (inset) Laura Cavanaugh/FilmMagic/
Getty Images; pp. 3, 6, 17, 27, 36, 44, 45 (background image) © iStockphoto.com/loops7; pp. 4–5
McClatchy-Tribune/Getty Images; p. 6 Steve Petteway/Collection of the Supreme Court of the United
States/AP; p. 7 Courtesy of the Office of the Bronx Borough President; p. 8 White House/AP Images;
p. 13 Otto Greule Jr./Getty Images; p. 15 Paul J. Richards/AFP/Getty Images; p. 17 Pete Souza/Official
White House Photo; p. 19 aimintang/E+/Getty Images; p. 20 Steve Petteway/Collection of the Supreme
Court of the United States; p. 23 Marilynn K. Yee/The New York Times/Redux; p. 25 Karen Bleier/AFP/
Getty Images; pp. 27, 29, 39 © AP Images; p. 35 Chip Somodevilla/Getty Images; p. 36 Paul Marotta/
Getty Images; p. 43 RJ Sangosti/Denver Post/Getty Images; cover and interior graphic elements ©
iStockphoto.com/BeholdingEye (rays), © iStockphoto.com/JSP007 (interior pages border pattern),
abstract/Shutterstock.com (silhouetted figures and map).

CONTENTS

INTROD

Sonia Sotomayor's story takes her from a poor neighborhood in the Bronx to the United States Supreme Court.

A little girl watches her mother go to work every day, working long, hard hours as a nurse. Her father is dead and her family is poor, and they live around other poor people. The little girl sees the adults in her neighborhood work tough jobs, like her mother. They do not wear suits and ties or nice dresses to work, and they usually work at very tiring, low-paying jobs.

Some people in the neighborhood get angry and impatient with such a difficult life and get in trouble with the law. This little girl will do just the opposite—instead of getting in trouble with the law, she will make the law her career. She will become a lawyer, then a judge, and eventually a member of the highest court in the United States. That little girl was named Sonia Sotomayor, and today she is an associate justice on the United States Supreme Court.

To make the journey from that apartment in the Bronx to the Supreme Court, Sonia had to overcome many difficulties. By doing that, she made her story an inspiration to many different types of people.

On June 25, 1954, a new baby was welcomed to the South Bronx. Juan and Celina Sotomayor named their new baby girl Sonia, a name that means "wisdom."

Juan and Celina Sotomayor had come to New York City when Celina was serving in the Women's Auxiliary Corps, a branch of the U.S. Army, during World War II. After Sonia, they had one other child, a boy who was named Juan after his father. The family was not very well off, and the Bronx was one of the poorer and rougher areas of New York. Still, the Sotomayor kids had

The interest in law that led Sotomayor to the Supreme Court has its roots in her childhood.

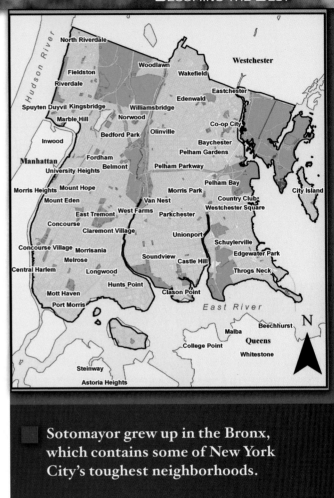

one advantage that was going to make a big difference in their lives—a mother who understood that getting an education was going to be the key to her children having a brighter future.

Sotomayor grew up in the Bronx, which contains some of New York City's toughest neighborhoods.

GETTING AN EDUCATION

Despite her mother's support, Sonia faced some challenges in getting an education. Her

father, a factory worker whose highest level of school had been the third grade, never really adjusted to speaking English regularly after moving from Puerto Rico. Spanish is the most common language in Puerto Rico, and in her early years, Sonia and her family spoke mostly Spanish around the house. Because of this, when Sonia went to school in New York City,

Her mother's insistence on getting an education and setting high standards started Sotomayor on the road to success.

she had to take her lessons in a language she did not regularly speak.

Language was not the only challenge Sonia faced. When she was seven, she found out that she had childhood diabetes. Then, when she was nine, her father died. This meant that her mother had to work long hours as a nurse to support the family, and they had to live in a public housing project.

Despite all those obstacles, Sonia's mother made sure her kids understood the importance of getting an education. She told them, "I don't care what you do, but be the best at it." Young Sonia took that advice seriously. She was the valedictorian, which is an honor for being the top student in one's class, in both grade school and high school.

QUICK FACT

As a student, Sonia Sotomayor won academic awards in grade school, high school, and college.

Her excellence in school earned Sonia something that would have been beyond the dreams of most people growing up in the South Bronx—a chance to go to college at Princeton University, one of the best schools in the country. Her mother did not have enough money to send her to such an expensive college, but Sonia's achievements in high school won her a scholarship to Princeton.

Though she had earned her place at a top-level school, Sonia found the adjustment to Princeton to be difficult at first. Having grown up around fellow Puerto Ricans and other Hispanics, Sonia found the mainly white student culture at Princeton to be unfamiliar, and the classwork was much harder than anything she had encountered before. However, she found a way to bridge the gap between her childhood world and Princeton. She joined Puerto Rican cultural and political groups on campus so she would feel in touch with her roots, but she also took extra English and writing classes so she could better communicate with the mainstream of U.S. culture.

The hard work paid off. Sonia not only earned a college degree from Princeton, but she also won high honors and awards for the quality of her work.

PURSUING A CAREER IN THE LAW

By now, Sonia Sotomayor had her eyes on a career in the law. She went to Yale to get a law degree, and then passed the New York State bar exam in 1980. Passing this exam qualified her to practice law, and she got a job as an assistant district attorney in New York City.

Assistant District Attorney Sotomayor was responsible for presenting cases against accused criminals in court. These cases often involved crimes that were violent, such as murders, robberies, and child abuse. It was a tough job, but her boss described her as a "fearless and effective prosecutor."

After five years as an assistant district attorney, Sotomayor got a job with Pavia & Harcourt, a law firm in Manhattan. Here, she practiced a very different kind of law, usually involving business issues. On top of her years

as a criminal prosecutor, dealing with business law gave Sotomayor a broader range of experience. This would serve her well in her next job, which was as a United States district court judge.

JUDGE SOTOMAYOR

In 1992, President George H.W. Bush appointed Sotomayor as a district court judge. This was an especially great honor for somebody of her age (she was still in her thirties). Sotomayor became the youngest U.S. district court judge at that time. It was as a district court judge that Sotomayor first came to national attention in 1995 with a ruling that helped end a dispute between Major League Baseball players and team owners—a dispute that had forced the cancellation of the World Series the year before. Sotomayor's ruling is generally credited with saving the 1995 season from being ruined as well.

This was just one of 450 cases Sotomayor dealt with in six years as a district court judge.

As a district court judge, Sotomayor first came to national attention when one of her rulings ended a baseball players strike.

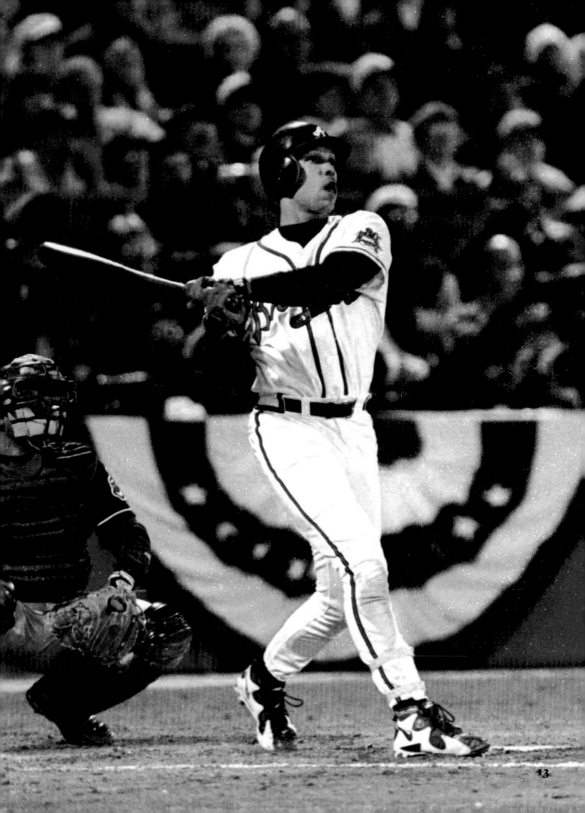

It was a demanding job, but as it had throughout her life, her hard work paid off. In 1998 Sotomayor was named to a higher federal court, the U.S. Court of Appeals for the Second Circuit.

The federal court system has three main levels. The lowest level is the district court, which is where federal cases are usually first heard. The second level is the court of appeals. These courts hear cases in which there might be a legal reason to rethink the decision of a district court. The next level after the court of appeals is the Supreme Court, the highest court in the United States. The Supreme Court consists of a chief justice

Sotomayor's mother and brother were with her when she was sworn in as a Supreme Court justice.

and eight associate justices. After her six years on the district court and nearly eleven on the court of appeals, Sotomayor was nominated by President Barack Obama to become one of those eight Supreme Court associate justices.

QUICK FACT

Sotomayor rose through all three levels of the federal court system: district court, court of appeals, and the Supreme Court.

When the Senate approved Sotomayor's nomination to the Supreme Court in 2009, she had reached the very top of the legal profession. With all her success, Sotomayor never forgot who was responsible for guiding her on this course—even after making it to the Supreme Court, Sotomayor still spoke to her mother on the phone almost every day.

CHAPTER 2

MAKING AN IMPACT

S onia Sotomayor has come a long way in life. She has had many different experiences— student, assistant district attorney, private lawyer, and judge—and has succeeded at all of them.

One reason for Sotomayor's success is that she has never been half-hearted about anything she has done. She has sought to make a clear impact at every stage of her life.

Sotomayor was nominated to become a U.S. Supreme Court justice in 2009 by President Barack Obama.

EYES ON THE PRIZE

Part of succeeding is knowing what one wants. Sotomayor set her sights on the legal profession at a very young age. When she first became a judge, people who had known her as a child wrote to let her know that they remembered her saying in grade school that she wanted to be a judge.

With the honors she won in grade school and high school, it is clear that Sotomayor took her goal of becoming a judge seriously. That enabled her to attend top colleges such as Princeton and Yale, which is not very common for people who grow up in housing projects. Sotomayor did not just attend these schools; she excelled at each one.

At Princeton, besides graduating with honors, she won the M. Taylor Pyne Prize, which is the school's highest award for any student earning an undergraduate degree. At Yale, Sotomayor became an editor of the *Yale Law Journal* and a managing editor of the *Yale Studies in World Public Order*.

After a difficult adjustment to college at first, Sotomayor made her mark at Princeton by winning a top academic honor.

At competitive schools such as Yale, winning a top job at this type of student publication is not only a big honor but also a way of having a voice in legal and public

By becoming an editor of the *Yale Law Journal*, Sotomayor was able to influence how people thought about the law.

Like Sotomayor, fellow Supreme Court justice Samuel Alito once edited the prestigious *Yale Law Journal*.

policy. The *Yale Law Journal* in particular is known around the world, so being its editor gives a person the chance to make an impact on how people view discussions about the law. The late Supreme Court justice Abe Fortas and current Supreme Court

justice Samuel Alito are other former editors of the *Yale Law Journal* who went on to become justices of the Supreme Court.

GIVING BACK

Academic achievements and a successful career are just two ways that Sotomayor has made an impact. She has also used her talents to try to help the communities of people living around her.

When lawyers volunteer their services, it is called pro bono work. There are many legal phrases still used today that are made up of Latin words, and "pro bono" is a common one. These words mean "for good," and in her years

QUICK FACT

Even while her career as a lawyer was on the fast track, Sotomayor took the time to donate her services to community efforts.

as a lawyer, Sotomayor earned a reputation as somebody who was willing to do pro bono work for the good of her community.

For example, Sotomayor spent twelve years as one of the leading policy makers for the board of the Puerto Rican Legal Defense and Education Fund. This organization tries to give young Puerto Ricans the resources they need to find careers in fields that can be difficult for people from poorer backgrounds to join.

Sotomayor also served on the board of the State of New York Mortgage Agency. This agency provides low-income housing projects and AIDS care facilities with the insurance necessary for them to get mortgages. In addition, Sotomayor helped start the New York City Campaign Finance Board, which distributes public money for political campaigns. The idea behind this organization is to make sure that candidates who do not have much private money behind them will be heard by voters as well.

When someone is nominated for the U.S. district court, the nomination needs to be

As a young, up-and-coming attorney in New York City, Sotomayor still took time to do community service work.

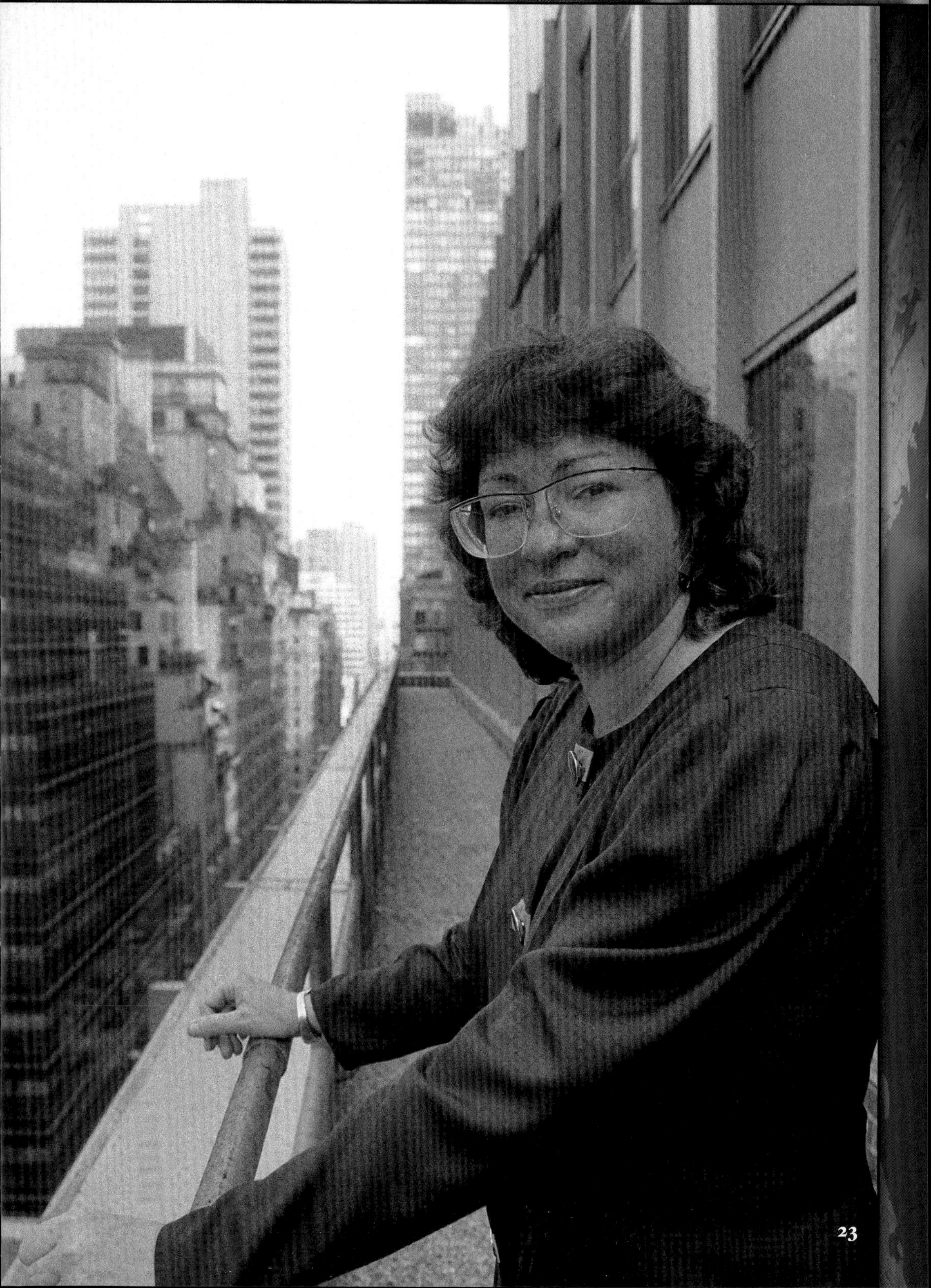

approved by the U.S. Senate. In the Senate hearings about Sotomayor's qualifications, veteran senator Edward Kennedy praised her for her long-time commitment to pro bono work. In trying to make a difference in her community, Sotomayor also impressed influential people who would have a say in her career.

High Qualifications for the High Court

Being named to the Supreme Court is a great honor that very few people achieve. It means that the person nominated has done exceptional work related to the law, whether

Quick Fact

Sotomayor not only earned the qualifications to be a Supreme Court justice, but she was one of the most experienced judges named to the court in the past century.

Her history of pro bono work helped Sotomayor make a good impression during Senate hearings on her Supreme Court nomination.

as a lawyer, judge, or teacher. Even by this high standard, Sotomayor brought to the Supreme Court qualifications that were above and beyond the norm for the high court.

With her seventeen years in total on the district court and court of appeals, Sotomayor had the most experience as a judge of anyone

named to the Supreme Court in seventy years, and the most experience as a federal judge of any Supreme Court justice in one hundred years. Her experience as an assistant district attorney and as a corporate lawyer further added to her exceptional qualifications.

By making an impact at everything she has done in school, work, and the community, Sotomayor has made it clear why she earned her appointment to the Supreme Court. It is not because of her politics, or because she is a woman, or because she is Hispanic. It is because she has a history of making a difference.

CHAPTER 3

BECOMING AN INSPIRATION

S onia Sotomayor is a classic American success story. She has risen from difficult beginnings to do great things. Her achievements have done more than just help her own career—they have made her an inspiration to others in a variety of ways.

Sotomayor knows about being inspired by someone. Her mother's emphasis on excellence and education helped set the stage for Sotomayor's outstanding academic career. As for what directed Sotomayor toward a legal career, that inspiration came from a different source—a television program.

Sotomayor's background and achievements make her an inspiration to young people from a variety of backgrounds.

Perry Mason was a popular television show in the 1950s and 1960s. It had a lead character who was an attorney, and much of the action was set in a courtroom. It was from watching this TV show as a child that young Sonia developed an interest in the law and gained an understanding of what a judge's job was.

Thanks to the inspiration of *Perry Mason*, the stage was set for Sotomayor's career and also for her to become, in turn, an inspiration to others—including women, Hispanics, people who want to rise from poverty, and anyone who is interested in the law.

AN INSPIRATION TO WOMEN

Although women represent slightly more than half the population of the United States, they have historically held relatively few positions of power, such as leading big companies, holding national political offices—or serving as Supreme Court justices.

The Supreme Court dates back more than two hundred years, and in all that time only four women have ever served on it. The first,

Justices Ginsburg, O'Connor, Sotomayor, and Kagan are the only women in history to have served on the Supreme Court.

Sandra Day O'Connor, was appointed in 1981 and retired in 2006. As of 2010, Sotomayor was one of just three women out of the total of nine Supreme Court justices. This not only put her in a position to bring a woman's perspective to key decisions but also helped demonstrate to others that women can succeed at one of the most demanding jobs in the country.

Sotomayor is one of just four women ever appointed to the Supreme Court, and as of 2014 was one of three women serving on the court.

Sotomayor understands the importance of making sure the nation's courts represent the interests of all segments of its population. Besides being a positive role model for women who want to be judges, as a court of appeals judge she served on the Second Circuit Task Force on Gender, Racial, and Ethnic Fairness in the Courts.

AN INSPIRATION TO HISPANICS

Sotomayor is proud of her Hispanic heritage, and in turn other Hispanics are able to take pride in her accomplishments.

More than sixteen out of every one hundred people in the United States is Hispanic, but in the past they have not often held positions of authority in the U.S. court system. Time after time, Sotomayor led the way in breaking down those traditional barriers.

Sotomayor was the first Puerto Rican to become a federal judge in New York City— a significant accomplishment in an area with a large Puerto Rican population. Later, she became the first woman with Latin American roots to serve on the U.S. Court of Appeals, and eventually she became the first Hispanic Supreme Court justice.

Besides leading by example, in college and as an attorney Sotomayor joined organizations dedicated to Puerto Rican causes. By keeping a clear connection with her ethnic roots, Sotomayor has helped people with similar backgrounds feel a part of her success. When she first became a judge she received letters from other Hispanics telling her that they were proud of her appointment.

Sotomayor thinks it is important for Hispanics to see one of their own sitting as

QUICK FACT

By breaking new ground for Hispanic representation at the district, appeals, and Supreme Court levels, Sotomayor has helped people with backgrounds like hers feel that they are more a part of the justice system.

a judge. She once told the *New York Times*, "I hope there's some greater comfort about the system to Hispanics because I'm there."

An Inspiration for People Wanting to Rise from Poverty

Being poor can become a cycle that goes on for generations: children in poor neighborhoods don't always have access to the best educational opportunities, so when they grow up they often have fewer job skills and have to take

lower-paying positions. This means their children grow up poor and repeat the cycle. It takes people like Sonia Sotomayor to come along now and then to show that with the right focus and determination the cycle can be broken.

When Sotomayor received an honorary degree from Pace University, the citation she received called her "a role model of aspiration, discipline, commitment, intellectual prowess and integrity." Sotomayor understands the importance of being a role model to young people who may have met few examples of professional success in their personal lives. She has participated in the Development School for Youth program, which brings inner city high school students together with successful people from a variety of fields for special workshops. In Sotomayor's case, she conducted legal workshops and had the students play different roles in a pretend trial. This first-hand exposure to what it is like to practice law may have sparked an interest in some of those students that will eventually lead to a career.

Sotomayor has tried to pass along her success by teaching law and conducting workshops for inner-city students.

AN INSPIRATION TO ANYONE INTERESTED IN THE LAW

It is easy to see how people who have grown up with some of the same challenges as Sotomayor might see a little of her in themselves, but a person does not have to be a woman, Hispanic, or from a poor family in order to take inspiration from her success. Anyone who is interested in a legal career can admire her passion for the law.

Sotomayor has tried to pass along that passion by teaching others. Prior to becoming

The U.S. Supreme Court has nine justices who are nominated by the president and confirmed by the Senate; here are the nine justices in 2010.

a Supreme Court justice, she was a lecturer at Columbia Law School and a part-time professor at New York University School of Law. With her multifaceted career, Sotomayor was able to demonstrate to these students that they can hope to go on to successful careers as public prosecutors, private attorneys, or judges—and possibly even Supreme Court justices.

Besides serving as a role model, Sonia Sotomayor holds a position as a Supreme Court judge, which allows her to directly affect even more lives by helping to shape the law of the land.

There are three main branches of the United States government: The legislative (Congress), the executive (the president), and the judicial (the court system). Congress formulates and passes laws, and the president can sign or veto those laws, as well as make decisions about how laws are carried out. The judicial branch has a crucial role to play in deciding how laws should be applied to specific situations.

Throughout her life, Sotomayor has received many honors for her academic, professional, and community activities.

For one thing, laws are often written in very general terms, and some are decades or even centuries old. They cannot anticipate every specific situation that might be an example of breaking that law, especially with changes in technology and culture over time. So courts have to decide how to interpret laws to fit specific situations.

Court decisions can also become what are known as legal precedents. These are interpretations of laws that not only fit the situation being decided for the court but also give guidance for how similar cases should be decided by other judges in the future. Precedents can be set at any level of the court

QUICK FACT

Judges at any level of the court system can influence how laws are interpreted and applied, so Sotomayor has helped shape United States law for over twenty years now.

system, but as a case moves up the levels of that system—from district courts to appeals courts to the Supreme Court—precedents carry greater weight.

Because of the importance of legal precedents, as one of nine Supreme Court justices Sonia Sotomayor has a strong voice in how the laws of the United States are interpreted and applied. Over the course of her career, Sotomayor has played a part in deciding some of the most important legal issues facing the country.

KEY LEGAL ISSUES

As a federal judge, Sotomayor has been involved in several decisions that could help shape United States law for decades to come.

QUICK FACT

The United States Supreme Court is the highest court in the land, so it has the strongest voice in deciding how laws should be interpreted and applied.

The following are just a few examples of issues affected by these decisions:

- Employee bargaining rights: Companies often have a lot of power over their employees. Because workers depend on employers for a job, workers are often in a weaker position when it comes to bargaining. To even things out, United States law allows workers to organize together to bargain as a group; this is known as collective bargaining. In her

In one of her influential decisions, Justice Sotomayor helped defend the rights of workers to negotiate with their employers. Here, representatives of auto workers (*left*) negotiate with executives of a large car company.

decision on the baseball strike, Sotomayor helped defend the rights of workers to be fairly represented when dealing with their employers.

- Individual rights: The government needs to be able to make and enforce laws, but sometimes these actions can conflict with the rights of individual citizens. As a district judge, Sotomayor ruled on a variety of cases in which she put limits on how far the government could go in restricting individual freedoms.

- Equal opportunity: For much of its history, the United States did not have laws that gave certain groups, such as ethnic minorities and women, equal protection of their opportunities to go to college or get good jobs. Since the civil rights movement of the 1960s, laws have been put in place to try to make up for this, but now some of those laws are being challenged before the Supreme Court. This is expected to cause a split between the more conservative and more liberal judges on the court, and Sotomayor is expected to argue in favor of laws that give certain groups preferred treatment to make up for past wrongs.

The nine Supreme Court justices vote on the decision for each case, and they do not always agree. Like each of the other justices, Sotomayor helps make sure that a variety of different points of view are heard when deciding on points of law.

• Voting rights: Some of the same groups that were once denied opportunities in education and jobs were also once prevented from voting freely. Laws were made to fix that problem, but some people feel that enough time has passed for those laws to no longer be necessary. As with equal opportunity, voting rights is an issue that closely divides the court, making each of the Supreme Court justices' opinions, on either side of the issue, all the more important.

• Right to privacy: Since the terrorist attacks of September 11, 2001, the U.S. government has stepped up its efforts to try to get information about other plots against the country and its people. Sometimes that involves spying on people within the country. This is another key issue that has come before the Supreme Court in Sotomayor's time on the court, and it is expected to be an issue that continues to come up in different ways in the future.

Because there are nine Supreme Court justices and decisions are made by voting, sometimes justices are on the winning side of those votes, and sometimes they are on the losing side. However, what is important is that each of those votes represents one of the many points of view on the issue, so having justices with differing opinions makes the court as a whole more representative of people in the country.

CONTINUING TO INSPIRE

Looking at Sonia Sotomayor's career from every angle shows that she has a history

Inspiring young people is just one of the ways that Justice Sotomayor has made a difference.

of making an impact in everything she has done academically and professionally. This success has made her a role model, especially because of her background. Beyond serving as an inspiration, Sotomayor also has a direct influence on the law of the United States in her position as a Supreme Court justice. She is clearly one of the notable persons who makes a difference in the early twenty-first century.

TIMELINE OF ACHIEVEMENTS

June 25, 1954: Sonia Sotomayor is born in the Bronx, New York.

1972: Sotomayor graduates as valedictorian of Cardinal Spellman High School.

1976: Sotomayor graduates summa cum laude from Princeton University.

1979: Sotomayor receives a Juris Doctor degree from Yale University.

1980: Sotomayor passes the New York State bar exam, entitling her to practice law.

1980: Sotomayor becomes an assistant district attorney in New York City.

1980: The Puerto Rican Legal Defense and Education Fund brings on Sotomayor as a member of its board.

1984: Sotomayor joins the private law firm of Pavia & Harcourt.

1987: Sotomayor becomes a member of the board of the State of New York Mortgage Agency.

1988: Sotomayor becomes a partner at Pavia & Harcourt.

1988: Sotomayor helps start the New York City Campaign Finance Board.

1992: President George H. W. Bush appoints Sotomayor as a U.S. district court judge.

1995: Sotomayor earns national attention when she decides a case to end a baseball strike.

1998: President Bill Clinton appoints Sotomayor to the U.S. Court of Appeals for the Second Circuit.

2009: Sotomayor is appointed by President Barack Obama to the U.S. Supreme Court.

- **Hillary Clinton.** Hillary Clinton became First Lady when her husband, Bill Clinton, was elected president, and she was an important political advisor to him. Later, she became a United States senator and then secretary of state in the Obama administration. She works with her husband and the Clinton Foundation to address a number of global issues.

- **Aung San Suu Kyi.** Aung San Suu Kyi is an activist who helped bring international attention to human rights violations in her native country of Burma (Myanmar). She was awarded the 1991 Nobel Peace Prize for her efforts.

- **Barack Obama.** In 2008, Barack Obama became the first African American to be elected president of the United States. He won reelection to a second term as president in 2012.

- **Sandra Day O'Connor.** In 1981, Sandra Day O'Connor was appointed by President Ronald Reagan as the first woman to serve on the United States Supreme Court. She served as a Supreme Court associate justice for twenty-five years.

- **John Roberts.** John Roberts was appointed as chief justice of the United States Supreme Court in 2005. He was the youngest person confirmed to that position since 1801.

civil rights The rights of personal liberty granted to United States citizens by the Thirteenth and Fourteenth Amendments to the Constitution and by acts of Congress.

collective bargaining Discussion between an employer and representatives of employees about wages, hours, and working conditions.

court of appeals The second level of the federal court system, where cases are heard if there is reason to believe the law was incorrectly applied in a lower court decision. There are twelve regional courts of appeals in the United States.

district court The starting level for the federal court system. There are ninety-four of these courts in the United States.

Hispanic Of, relating to, or being a person living in the United States whose ancestors lived in Latin America.

judge A public official having authority to decide questions brought before a court.

lawyer A person whose profession is to conduct lawsuits for clients, defend clients in legal proceedings, or advise about legal rights and obligations.

legal precedent A court decision that may serve as an example or rule to be followed in the future.

pro bono work Actions taken at no charge for the public good.

scholarship Money given to a student to help pay for his or her education.

supreme court The highest court in any political unit; therefore, there are various state supreme courts throughout the United States, but there is only one federal Supreme Court.

valedictorian The student usually of the highest rank in a graduating class who gives the farewell speech at graduation ceremonies.

BOOKS

Felix, Antonia. *Sonia Sotomayor: The True American Dream*. New York, NY: Berkley Trade, 2011.

Greenhouse, Linda. *The U.S. Supreme Court: A Very Short Introduction*. New York, NY: Oxford University Press, 2012.

O'Connor, Sandra Day. *Out of Order: Stories from the History of the Supreme Court*. New York, NY: Random House, 2013.

Schneider, Deborah, and Gary Belsky. *Should You Really Be a Lawyer?: The Guide to Smart Career Choices Before, During & After Law School*. Seattle, WA: Lawyer Avenue Press, 2010.

Sotomayor, Sonia. *My Beloved World*. New York, NY: Knopf, 2013.

Williams, Zella. *Sonia Sotomayor: Supreme Court Justice* (Hispanic Headliners). New York, NY: Powerkids Press, 2010.

Winter, Jonah. *Sonia Sotomayor: A Judge Grows in the Bronx/La juez que creció en el Bronx*. New York, NY: Atheneum Books for Young Readers, 2009.

WEBSITES

Because of the changing nature of Internet links, Rosen Publishing has developed an online list of websites related to the subject of this book. This site is updated regularly. Please use this link to access the list:

http://www.rosenlinks.com/mad/soto

*This book was purchased
with funds from a
generous donation by*

Dr. Kathryn W. Davis